My Path

I0164560

Copyright © 2018 by Courtland Morrison
All rights reserved. This book or any portion
thereof
may not be reproduced or used in any manner
whatsoever
without the express written permission of the
publisher
except for the use of brief quotations in a book
review.

Printed in the United States of America

CA Morrison Publishing, 2018

ISBN 978-0999612828

CA Morrison Publishing
www.courtlandmorrison.com

This book is dedicated to military professionals of the past, present, and future. To my Grandmother Mable Gillespie may she rest in peace and know that she is forever loved and missed. Yet her strength continues to persevere through all her children's, children and grandchildren.

Introduction

Welcome to my second chapter as a poet. I would like to acknowledge all who've supported me as I published my book "First Steps". My Path will be similar to my debut book, but I will bring out some of my early poetic pieces and present some of my new works. I invite you to experience my growth and in my writing style.

Thank you giving me a chance to share with you my unique blessing!!

Glory

I look up I see the glory of the sun and blue skies
above
I have the feeling of euphoria of being able to see
another sunrise To God be the glory how he has
blessed me again

The trials and tribulations we all must go through
is it not a humbling factor to know you are always
blessed?
To have a savior who you can speak to in any
second, minute, or hour
To have a savior that says bring all your troubles to
him, to have faith the size of a mustard seed, and
know he will see's all, hears all and knoweth all

What a power and love our Savior has that he can
heal the sick, feed the poor, and give everlasting
life to those who confess him as their savior

I look up at the sky and see the glory of the sun
and blue skies above I have the feeling of euphoria
of being able to see another sunrise

My Path

To God be the glory he blesses me continually
To God be the glory I worship Thee
Amen, Amen and Amen

My Path

A Small Taste

A small taste a piece of grace
I experience every day just to wake up and give
my lord his grace

His grace and mercy to sleep
Through the night and awaken from slumber
To have a shelter over my head and cloth to cover
my body

To feel the vibrations of the world around me, to
hear the birds overhead, to smell fresh honey from
a bee's hive

We are so blessed, yet we are so ignorant of these
small gracious things

We must be like a child and learn to appreciate
For what the Lord gives us everyday

That small taste that piece of grace we experience
every day, we must cherish and store it in our
minds and souls as a reminder we are
tremendously blessed every day

My Path

A Poem of Thanks

The beauty of the sun is warmth to my vision
As the clouds passed overhead
The chasm of wind furls at low

Yet I feel a presence of warmth, comfort, and
strength that surrounds me
I can hear the strength of his voice through nature's
gentle course
I can only admire the vision that he gave me
through evolutions discourse

The beauty of love and wisdom he portrays every
day is a finite vision
I humble myself before thee
How can I as a man, human born in his image
forsake him?

He has given so much
So, I can worship him every day
Protection during the night slumber, Breath into
my lungs, Nutrition for my body

The only answer I can say is thank you
For all the blessings he has given, and that is
forthcoming

I will emulate his precious word that he bestowed
upon our hearts

My Path

I thank him every day until my last breath taken till
I return from which I was brought
My Lord, Savior Jesus Christ I thank you for my
life, family, and friends always

My Path

I walk by faith not by sight

I walk by faith not by sight
For my physical eyes are skewed by depth and
perception
My spiritual eyes are more in depth of what my
Savior wants me to see

Do not struggle, do not feel anguish, For the Lord
has opened doors, sent you blessings, and has
given angels to protect you

Your physical eyes are just physical
They are for you to see the magnificence of beauty
God has created

I walk by faith not by sight
For my faith is what keeps me, holds me, and
strengthens me
In all my burdens, trials and tribulations he always
there to guide me and carry me

My foundation my cornerstone
My faith in the almighty
My sight defined

My Path

When I lost my voice, my words spoke to me

When I lost my voice, my words spoke to me
Your voice is so important to you
How are you defined without your voice?

My words replaced my voice
Words are soluble and dramatic
My words come from my heart and give me
Freedom of expression and intuition

Words give me the intelligence to think through
situations
To give you my thoughts of love and anger
To give you hope and compassion

The thought of losing my voice was scary but it
Actually, was a blessing in disguise
When I lost my voice, it punctuated my words
To convey my thoughts and dreams clearer

My Path

Patience

Be patient, Young man. For it's one of Gods great
virtues.
Patience is a strong and moral ground to be
thankful
Learn to be knowledgeable and be wise

Do not drop yourself and busy. Wise counsel is
always by your side.
Observation, slow to react, are truthful acts which
God has endeared.
Listening and speaking is a gratitude. One who
listens more and speaks less
gets more attention than the other. For those that
speak when is given the opportunity
people will focus on more of the words they share.

Be patient young man. Learn and develop one's
self.
Faith and divinity go hand in hand.
Knowledge and wisdom are power.

Be patient, Young man, be patient
Patience is a virtue

My Path

**My past has not defined me, destroyed me,
deterred me, or defeated me; it has only
strengthened me.**

It has defined the scars that have shaped me,
molded me,
to the person I am today
I will not be defeated nor brought down for my
victory has already begun
Deterrence is a naysayer which only inspires me to
push forward
My past is my past which has good times and bad
times yet
also points me to the future which is prominent in
my eyes and dreams

I am strengthened always in my faith, in my love,
in my spirit
The legacy of my life is already set
I just go through the journeys and trials as a
lifelong adventure of reading a great book or
watching a character make their way to a
dangerous trial

My Path

My past has not defined me, destroyed me,
deterred me, or defeated me; it has only
strengthened me
Strengthened me in mind, body, and soul
The past is my reflection of the old me to the new
you I see today

My Convictions

My convictions are numerous the truths are so few
A statement of growth is what I extend to
The depth of my passions and the intuition of my
soul is fire

I stake a claim what is mine and mine alone
I do not partake in this without a loss
For I will have stand alone and accept the actions
to come

The trials to come are just but an epithet for I am
weaned to hear
For in my heart there is an ever-growing fire that
will drown out the noise but give life to song and
grace

This constitution of words are the hymns of praise
That give my subconscious the victory I stream in
my heart

My convictions are the banner or the streamer I
carry in my heart
It gives me joy, laughter, and serenity to be me
The hopes and dreams I carry forward with me and
beyond

My Path

One Pen One pad

One pen, one pad
A poet's tools they live by
Eloquent words conceived in the heart
Process in the cerebral cortex

Flow like water with the movement of your hand
Pen in hand, Control of fingers,
Inscription of pen to pad
Adjectives and nouns objectified

Critiqued into a concept, layered pattern
A symphony of words scripted to
Scrap or pad

One pen, one pad
A poet's tools they live by
There legacy developed
Life defined

Concepts

The moonlight I spit at you; will not
clear
The darkness within you
I can't seem to light your vision & push you to see
the truth Therefore, the truth was never in you

The sun brightens my way toward you,
For the light of my eyes balances me speaking to
you The heart of your spirit combines my mental
which is knowledge that reigns supreme over me
and gives me light and visions you

Fiery Gods can't obtain water in the soul of
unrighteousness
You can never tell from a physical; spiritual;
energy is vague never sun and yourself by the
physical

Emotional yours the spirit of Jesus keeps my
affection when I met you
The blessings are so many which I wonder why
people want to go away from him
For he gives me the energy, physical, mental,
attributes that stabilizes me emotionally to keep
going to see the truth in you

Renata Smith & Courtland Morrison

Afro American History

A history of the historical origin
Long and treasured yet forgotten
A cultural heritage of riches
more plentiful than fish in the ocean
Yet more expensive than the largest diamond

A diversity of unequal parallel
A time of despair, A time of triumph
A time of fear, A time of joy

The Afro-American heritage a history
which should be recorded in all books
a revered culture for all people to know
The Afro-American history
Be proud of our heritage

The Land of Iraq

Iraq the birthplace of mankind, civilization
The land of Iraq combination of many facets
Deserts, mountainous regions, built-up towns
impoverished cities various aspects of land in Iraq

Lands of Iraq surreal in beauty, tranquil in mystic
Arid deserts parched over millenniums by the fiery
sun hilltops and mountainous region carved by
man and nature dried up rivers of old carving
complex landscapes in the foothills and valleys
giving similar results of Americas
vivid land piece of The Grand Canyon

Man to defend and fight against invading
neighbors from the great nation known in
Babylonian times as Persia
Bustling towns and cities all over
street markets, street vendors buzzing like bees
trading goods for money

Distinctive woven fabrics made to wear varied
hues in one's light of a vision delicate our sense of
touch

The land of Iraq remarkable in great books of
religion
Islam and Christianity intertwined in many of
people's faith

My Path

Islam the dominating religion of Iraq but just like
Christianity divided in two distinct groups

People of Iraq of various ethnicities,
Kurdish in the northern sector
Turkoman sprinkled in the north and all around
Arabs mixed all around

Iraq the birthplace of civilization and mankind
A unique kinship of land, people, and culture
Iraq a revered nation for eternity

My Path

A Poem to My Father from A Son Faraway

My father,
The man who christened me as his son
The one who gave me my name

My father,
The man who taught me right from wrong
The man who pushed me to exceed and go for my
wildest dreams

My father
The man of the house and protector his family

My father
Who taught me from a boy to be a man
To elevate where he left off

My father,
Who gave me many talents and taught me various
experiences

My father,
The man who brought me into this world
Who taught me right from wrong

These words I dedicate to you
Because you made me the man I am today
I love you

A poem to my father from his son who is far away

A Soldier experiencing PTSD

I sit alone, and I cry
For in the darkness I feel safe
This terrible disease I have keeps me trapped
The depression and anxiety forces people
To look at me, speak to me, and act towards me
In a half hazard way

I have seen anguish despair and martyrdom
Yet it feels like a new normal to me
All this pain and suffering only a few can
recognize

I sometimes wonder can I really do what I say I
can do? Did I answer the question correctly?
Nightmares scare me from a gentle slumber
Self-doubt and extreme bouts of anger in jest me

I ask please oh heavenly father help me to get
through this struggle and let me not be troubled by
this pain no more and help me have joy, spirit, and
happiness I crave for

A Rite of Passage

A poet's rite of passage unique to oneself
A passage that can go many ways
The usage of words, thought of emotion,
points of view, are thrust like a hurricane

 It turns, it churns and starts to take shape
Benevolent winds, crashing waves, torrid
winds blow and furl
The center of confusion so calm and gentle
Light but steady breeze, birds chirping,
A summers night in the evening

Usage of words, points of view,
thoughts of emotion finally form into an object
The object is passed and viewed with a delicate
eye

The hurricane is tracked and traced from formation
to possible landfall
Results of the poem are quantified and interpreted
Given review after review

Hurricane makes landfall
Torrential rains upon the landscape
Horrid cracks of lighting
Benevolent winds thrust about
A poet's rite of passage
Like a Hurricane goes on and on

The First Time I Looked into Your Eyes

The first time I looked into your eyes
It was like a waterfall flowing from a remote
mountain top
The sprouting of a rose from the earth for a new
day

The first time I looked into your eyes
It was the musical harmonies of Bach and
Beethoven describing your beauty
Yet the painters Leonardo and Michelangelo
painting your fluent curvature

The first time I looked in to your eyes
Your eyes transfixed me to one's soul
a sensory overload which overtook me
Your eyes hypnotized my thoughts only on you
The reason why I think of you and your beautiful
eyes
for I will always love you

Beauty in Motion

Beauty in your hands my love for a lifetime
You are my essence of beauty in motion
A soliloquy of the sunset on the beach
Beauty in motion

My love of a lifetime, you are the beat of my heart
water to my soul
The movement of clouds and the gracefulness of
your walk
the boundless energy if love and soul
Beauty in motion

Your face the likeness of Janet, gracefulness of
Dorothy Dandridge
the smile of Aaliyah, the eyes of Lela Rochon,
tenaciousness of Vivica Fox
Beauty in motion

Beauty in your hands my love of a lifetime
The essence of love in my heart, you are the
essence of grace
For therefore you are my Valentine
Because you are my beauty in motion

My Path

I Miss You

Your life is so precious, is why I love you so much
The beauty of your eyes, sweetness of your touch
is the memory I have of you
I miss you

I miss all the little things that we do together
Looking into your beautiful brown eyes is the glow
of the sun that reminds every day of you
Softness of your hands, delicate touch of your skin
Sweetness of your lips, reminds me of you so
I miss you

Sitting in the park just talking to you
Holding you close to me and just feeling
your body against me entrances me to you
I miss you

Baby I miss you so much
you mean the world to me
So many things I want to say
So, when my time is done, I want to spend
as much time as I can with you
With that said, girl the love I have for you'
is so precious, that's why I miss you so much
I miss you

My Path

Brown Eyes

I have seen you from afar and near
I wanna speak to you but my heart does not want
to break again

Your beautiful brown eyes draw me to you
Your smile and mannerisms are so sweet
Its no wonder I am attracted to you

You always encourage me, yet I lose my thoughts
and voice when I speak to you
My true feelings I want to convey will bring tears
to your eyes
I can't breathe for the moment I met you a change
in my life occurred
I can see my dreams and they are portrayed with
you
I want to make you smile when you are down,
wipe your tears and tell you everything will be
alright, I want to be like the sun because it's the
first to see you

One breath is what it will take for me to please you
I want you to know I will be here for you and your
kids
I just want an opportunity to show you what I can
do

I know you have been hurt in the past,
I want to be your future not your dream

My Path

I don't want to be your friend, I want to be your
husband

I feel you are the rib that was taken from me by
God
You are the woman I have been waiting for that
God has made you just for me

Give me the opportunity to be the man that I know
I can be for you

A Soldiers Heart

Friends of many envy of few
Praise, honor, and loyalty, empathy, of others
People of many creeds & religions, selfish of few
Brotherly kindness and loyalty, Jealously of others

The men who grew from boys with you
Loyalty and duty bonds, you for life
United for one common cause
Values of many organization, strong willed
fighters

Many branches, detailed to a common cause
Four specific, the spear of the sword
The other forty in support
The bond that keeps them together
their friendship, love of country, and love for each
other

Dedicated to US Armed Forces
Army, Marine Corps, Air Force, Navy, Coast
Guard

My Path

My Grandmother

My grandmother the rose of our family
The strength and queen who showed love
Compassion

She always encouraged and sent love
She was a mother, grandmother, great
Grandmother, and Great great grandmother

She loved cooking, music, going for rides
She was a religious woman who encouraged all
To have a relationship with our Lord and savior
Jesus Christ

My grandmother gave me so many memories
I don't remember where to start and nor where to
end
I know my grandmother is looking down on us and
her
Is smiling
I love you grandma

About the Author

Courtland Morrison is a man who served his country. To others, he is a quiet, humble, and a hard worker. While in the military these skills helped him rank as Sergeant. Courtland has always had a love of writing. However, it wasn't until he attended Georgia Military College his passion for the written word blossomed. During his tours in Iraq, he began writing to relieve his stress from combat and it allowed him to express himself. It wasn't long before his fellow soldiers had him writing notes of love for their significant others.

When Courtland is not writing he likes to read, be around friends and family, listen to music, go to car events.

www.ingramcontent.com/pod-product-compliance
Lightning Source LLC
Chambersburg PA
CBHW030011040426
42337CB00012BA/740